God's Christmas Presence—Copyright ©2021 by Katy Allen
Published by UNITED HOUSE Publishing

All rights reserved. No portion of this book may be reproduced or shared in any form–electronic, printed, photocopied, recording, or by any information storage and retrieval system, without prior written permission from the publisher. The use of short quotations is permitted.

New American Standard Bible®, Copyright © 1960, 1971, 1977, 1995, 2020 by The Lockman Foundation. All rights reserved.

ISBN: 978-1-952840-27-2

UNITED HOUSE Publishing
Waterford, Michigan
info@unitedhousepublishing.com
www.unitedhousepublishing.com

Cover and interior illustrations: Brenda Waraniak
Cover and interior formatting: Matt Russell, Marketing Image, mrussell@marketing-image.com

Published in Waterford, MI
Printed in the United States

2021—First Edition

SPECIAL SALES
Most UNITED HOUSE books are available at special quantity discounts when purchased in bulk by corporations, organizations, and special-interest groups. For information, please e-mail orders@unitedhousepublishing.com

To Noah, Belle, and Graham, my most precious gifts from God. Without you I would not have had the opportunity to see God's Gifts quite as clearly. And to Chris, my beloved husband. Thank you for grasping this vision and for welcoming this tradition into our family with such enthusiasm. Thank you for maintaining such a beautiful heart of worship. To Mom and Dad for planting seeds in my childhood to see and love Christ Jesus at Christmastime.

It was Christmas 2010. Our oldest son was eight years old, our daughter was three, and our youngest son was a year old. We were scraping to give our children a nice, memorable Christmas. To most children, that means presents. In order to offer more than one gift to each kid, we visited our local thrift store after hitting Walmart. We were stretching our dollars as far as we could. My husband and I were pleased with our purchases and just knew the kids would be thrilled too!

Christmas day arrived. Excitement was in the air. Our Christmas morning tradition was to read the Christmas story from Luke chapter two before giving presents. As per our ongoing giving tradition, we brought the gifts out to each child in turn. To my utter shock and dismay, after the last gift was unwrapped, I heard the words no parent wants to hear: "Is that all?" My heart broke at those three little words. It was at that moment I knew something had to change.

Why did my children have such high expectations of what they would get on Christmas morning? Truthfully, they were only being products of the culture. Christmas is so gift-oriented, especially in the United States. Think about it: what does everybody ask the kids at Christmas time? "What do you want for Christmas?" or, "What did you ask Santa to bring you for Christmas?" We needed to equip our children to see the value in what was in front of them, what was inside of them, and what the deeper meaning of the holiday afforded them. I needed to be more intentional in imparting these values. I needed a new perspective—a change of heart myself.

The custom of gift-giving comes from the Biblical account of the Wise Men who brought gifts to Jesus when He was a child. The Bible says, "...and they fell to the ground and worshipped Him. Then, opening their treasures, they presented to Him gifts of gold, frankincense, and myrrh" (Matthew 2:11). They worshipped Him. The gifts were presented in an act of worship to the Son of God, the King of kings, Emmanuel, God with us! He is God's gift to humankind. The custom of giving presents was to celebrate that gift and to remind each other of the precious gift God the Father gave to us through the birth of His Son, Jesus. It's all about Jesus Christ. That became the fire in my heart—that we would refocus on the original Gift and worship Him as we gave presents as a reminder of that first Christmas.

Back to that fateful morning.
"Not ever again!" I promised myself. I began contemplating possibilities for the next Christmas, and I asked Holy Spirit to help me see what the change needed to be and how to make it happen. Without a fresh perspective, the Christmas holiday was in danger of being banned from the Allen household!

I am not against presents at Christmas. I am one of the biggest fans of gifts—giving and receiving! I love gifts. I will never be a person who turns down a gift, especially something that smells good or glitters! There is also nothing like the thrill of giving someone a gift you put your heart into to bring them happiness. I am a kid at heart when it comes to Christmas and birthdays. However, I believe we desperately need a shift in the focus and priority of this holiday. This day was meant to be set aside in remembrance of the Son of God coming to Earth, but instead, I always grew weary and ended the day feeling less than satisfied—empty even. I believe that longing for a deep, spiritual moment on a day reserved to remember a Heaven-touching-Earth event for mankind is natural, but it takes work to give it the recognition it deserves. It is simply not in our human nature to look past the material gifts and dwell on something that took place so long ago.

We had included, as part of our annual tradition, taking gifts to people who had more physical needs to be met as a family. However, we knew we could not simply stop there. To give of oneself merely to help someone in need, lessen the stress of another, or lighten the load of a neighbor is an essential part of the journey of a believer. These acts open our hearts to the Savior and the way He sees the world and us. It is a way to allow Him to use us, and in turn, watch Him do miracles with our hands as we extend them in faith. To limit this only to Christmas time was robbing my kids of a very important aspect of our practical faith. It wasn't getting the deeper message of the season through to them. Therefore, we looked to expand those acts of kindness to everyday occurrences. I believe the Lord was trying to show me something more. I was seeking Him for more. I wanted something creative, yet meaningful, that would include children and adults alike. I wanted a new tradition that made Him the main focus.

"Our job as a parent is to reflect the heart of Father God as best as we can in our human state so our children will have less baggage when they become adults," was something we heard early in our marriage and took to heart. Although I'm not completely sure when this wisdom was imparted to us, we knew we wanted to apply it to our parenting. We shared a common desire to establish a strong family unit. We wanted to raise children that would be emotionally healthy, mentally stable, and full of faith and love for God.

Each generation builds on what the previous generation built, and it goes on and on and on. I am thankful our parents instilled in us many wonderful attributes like faith, family, and giving hearts. We were blessed with a heritage of godliness. However, no matter how faithful and godly, each generation is human. Each one carries brokenness. If it were not so, we wouldn't need Jesus! As our family grew, we began unpacking our own ideas and perspectives about life and what it meant to be a Christian family.

So, I began with a goal to see Christmas as Father God would view it. The Word of God says our Heavenly Father gives good gifts. Matthew 7:11 says, "If you then, being evil, know how to give good gifts to your children, how much more will your Father who is in heaven give what is good to those who ask Him!" We also see in James 1:17 that "every good thing given and every perfect gift is from above, coming down from the Father of lights." I asked myself, "When does He give these gifts? He doesn't wait until one day of the year to give to us. He is giving all of the time."

I tell my kids if they can't find anything to be thankful for, start with little things like the shoes on their feet. It took a little while to realize all the things we took for granted were actually gifts from God—such as a bed to sleep in, a car that runs, a healthy family, food in our kitchen, a livable income, the ability to think and reason, clothes on our back, clean drinking water, colors, flowers, seasons… the list goes on. We began to understand everything in our life is from the hand of our loving, gracious, and compassionate Father God. It is a constant flow. He is the Giver, the reason we celebrate and our attention should be on Him.

I could not shake the revelation that He is giving all of the time. He is giving all of the time! We often miss so many of the things God gives us because we can't see that God is giving to us constantly. That was when I knew what I wanted to do. Being inspired by this revelation, I purchased some decorative boxes and designated each one to a specific thing that we recognized as a "Gift from God" for the current year. This required us to look around at the precious little things the Lord blessed us with on a daily basis. Each family member that was able to articulate gratitude would deposit a written description in each box of how that particular thing was a gift to them that year.

What happened that next Christmas was astounding and wonderful!

On Christmas morning of 2011, before any other gift was opened, we opened God's Gifts. We read each slip of paper expressing our thankfulness and acknowledging the goodness of God, and He showed up! The presence of the Lord was so sweet in our home that morning-and has continued every Christmas morning since! After we finished going through God's Gifts, our hearts were so full that one of my children even said, "I don't need to open anything else!" That was it. That was what I had always imagined Christmas to be.

Here is how you can experience God's Christmas Presence in your home.

STEP 1
Determine the categories your family feels are the gifts God blessed you with this year. For example, we usually have 6 boxes: Family, Church, Job, School, Car, House, and always Jesus. These are subject to change based on the events of the year (i.e. a raise, new house, healing, etc.).

STEP 2
Purchase or make decorative boxes with lids that you will label for each category or "gift". We use boxes that do not require wrapping and reuse them each Christmas.

STEP 3
Label each box like so:
Employment
From: God
To: Us or The Family

STEP 4
Place the boxes together in a special and prominent place that's easy to see and access. We put ours under the tree because that tends to attract a lot of attention. We keep the other presents in a hidden place.

STEP 5
For several days leading up to Christmas, each member of the family writes how each gift has blessed them this year. For instance, I would write on a small piece of paper, "The Smith's provided dinner for us when I was recovering from surgery in May." Then, I would put it in the Church or Friends gift box. My son might write, "John is always helping me with my homework. That makes me feel special" and put it in the Family gift box. We usually start our boxes on December 12th. The time to begin is entirely up to you and your family. The goal is to have several papers in each gift box by Christmas morning.

STEP 6
On Christmas morning, before any other presents are opened, gather the God's Gifts boxes with your family. Open each box, tell which gift it is, then begin to read each slip of paper one by one. By the time you finish reading the last paper from the last box, your hearts will be full!

I pray your God's Gifts experience revolutionizes your Christmas in the same way it did ours. May Heaven touch your hearts this holiday season in ways you never imagined!

Merry Christmas!

About the Author:

Katy Allen is a wife, mother, singer, worshipper, and Director of Children's Ministry at her church. Having spent over 30 years involved in leading people into the presence of the Lord through music, she is branching out into using the written word. She has been active in church all of her life, participating in worship teams, in leadership roles, and on church staff. She fell in love with Jesus at the age of thirteen and has been passionate about His presence ever since. Katy loves to travel and experience new cultures. She and her family lived a short time in Berlin, Germany, where her youngest child was born. She believes there's no such thing as too much color or tea. She loves flying kites, playing Chinese checkers, and observing nature. She lives with her husband, two of her three children (her oldest has just gone off to college), and small dog in Ennis, Texas.

About the Illustrator:

Traverse City, MI artist **Brenda Waraniak**, has been honing her art skills for over 30 years. Originally a graphic designer, turned art teacher and illustrator, she finds her inspiration in her faith and in nature. Brenda enjoys working in watercolor, acrylic and oil paints but still enjoys creating designs in Adobe Illustrator and photoshop. She has worked for companies such as Michaels, Hobby Lobby, Hirschberg Schultz and Meteor Photo Co.

www.ingramcontent.com/pod-product-compliance
Lightning Source LLC
Chambersburg PA
CBHW041229240426

43673CB00010B/285